NONE OF THIS IS PROBABLY TRUE

NONE OF THIS IS PROBABLY TRUE

John Wing Jr.

mosaic press

National Library of Canada Cataloguing in Publication Data

Wing, John, 1959-
None of this is probably true

Includes index.
ISBN 0-88962-790-8

I. Title.

PS8595.I5953N65 2002   C811'.54   C 2002-900975-8
PR9199.3.W4992N65 2002

No part of this book — may be reproduced or transmitted in any form, by any means, electronic or mechanical, including photocopying and recording, information storage and retrieval systems, without permission in writing from the publisher, except by a reviewer who may quote brief passages in a review.

Published by Mosaic Press, offices and warehouse at 1252 Speers Road, Units 1 and 2, Oakville, Ontario, L6L 5N9, Canada and Mosaic Press, PMB 145, 4500 Witmer Industrial Estates, Niagara Falls, NY, 14305-1386, U.S.A.

Mosaic Press acknowledges the assistance of the Canada Council and the Department of Canadian Heritage, Government of Canada for their support of our publishing programme.

Copyright © 2002 John Wing Jr.,
Printed and Bound in Canada.
ISBN 0-88962-790-8

Mosaic Press in Canada:
1252 Speers Road, Units 1 & 2,
Oakville, Ontario
L6L 5N9
Phone/Fax: 905-825-2130
mosaicpress@on.aibn.com

Mosaic Press in U.S.A.:
4500 Witmer Industrial Estates
PMB 145, Niagara Falls, NY
14305-1386
Phone/Fax: 1-800-387-8992
mosaicpress@on.aibn.com

Le Conseil des Arts   The Canada Council
   du Canada   for the Arts

www.mosaic-press.com

CHARLES ANDREW WING, 1865 - 1916,
WHOSE STORY INSPIRED ME,

CLARENCE AUCKLAND WING, 1900 - 1992,
WHO KNEW IT ALL AND NEVER TOLD.

TABLE OF CONTENTS

INTRODUCTION	**IX**
ANOTHER NATURE	**1**
RISEN	3
I WILL	4
FIRST KNOCK	5
SECOND KNOCK	6
BIRTHDAY POEM	7
CHOICES	8
TALK SHOW	9
BOOK SIGNING	11
INTERMISSION	12
HIGH FIDELITY	13
THE JOHN	14
OLD HABITS	15
WHAT I TELL YOU THREE TIMES IS TRUE	**17**
THEN EVEN NOW	19
ELBOW-ROTIC	21
LICENSE RENEWAL	22
HOLLYWOOD	23
THE CHEETAH	24
IMMORTALITY ON THE ROAD TO EDMONTON	25
LETTER TO THE CHILDREN FROM THE ROAD	26
RACHEL, AGED EIGHT	27
FULMINATE	28
NUMEROLOGY	30
MOTHER AT AIR CANADA CENTER	31
TWO IS NONE	**33**
BLUES FOR A SMALL ROOM	35
NEW PAJAMAS	36
TAKEN DOWN AND USED AS EVIDENCE	37
NEW SKINS	38
TIMEBENDS	39
FANTASIES	40
INVINCIBLE	41

HALF THE KNOWN WORLD	42
EVEREST	43
UNTIL THEN	44
DESCRIBING HER IN TERMS OF SEA LIFE	45
HOME COMING	46

NONE OF THIS IS PROBABLY TRUE — 47

INTERVIEW	49
PREFACE	51
TWO HISTORIES	52
SECRETS	55
DWELLINGS	56
CLUES	57
INNOVATOR	58
UNCLE CHARLIE'S BLUES	59
JUXTAPOSITION	62
ORPHANS	63
PREDICTION	64
REAL REASONS	65
THE LOVER'S SONG	66
RIVALS	67
RECIPE	69
ROOTS OF INSOMNIA	70

ACKNOWLEDGEMENTS — 73

INTRODUCTION

A word that describes me well is *slow*. I see very little that occurs in front of me. I didn't realize my grandmother was an alcoholic until after she was dead. I didn't realize I was a drug addict until I'd been one for over ten years. I have accused people of many things, only to find out I was guilty of similar crimes. I have stated things I thought were true and, when they turned out to be true, I was crushed. Nothing is more embarrassing than personal revelation.

This book was written from back to front, more or less. I began with the story of my great-great Uncle's insanity. Charles Andrew Wing was a farmer who, according to the legend, lost his entire family over a couple of months in the influenza pandemic of 1920. The loss drove him insane and he spent the rest of his life in an asylum. That was the tale, and it stayed with you. Utterly tragic, perfectly reasonable, and not necessarily true.

In the mid 1980's I was traveling around, searching out Wing family gravesites in Southern Ontario. I asked my grandfather, Charlie's nephew, if he knew where Charlie was interred, or the name of the asylum. "We don't talk about Charlie," was all Grandpa would say about it, then or ever. My father, who had heard the influenza story when he was a boy, suggested that Grandpa was still too embarrassed to talk about the mental illness of a close relative. That it was taboo when he was a boy. The embarrassment aspect of the story was probably true. Shame might even be a better word.

Eight years after Grandpa died I found Charlie's grave right where it should have been, in the main cemetery in Rodney, Ontario. A couple of months before, a researcher friend had suggested that the London Asylum, which had once been visited by Walt Whitman, no less, was obviously the place to which Charlie would have been committed. He wrote for the medical file and soon I had the whole story. Charlie had died in 1916, three years before the flu pandemic that didn't harm a hair on his family's head. He had entered the asylum in 1909, a textbook case of paranoid schizophrenia, although that diagnosis was unknown at the time.

Most of the file comprised of letters to the Superintendent from family members, mostly his wife, inquiring as to Charlie's condition, which did not change until late in 1915 when he developed pulmonary tuberculosis, whereupon he wasted away and died in October of 1916. He had two shirt collars, one pair of socks, one pair of pants, one pair of shoes, one shirt, and one pair of underwear. He weighed eighty pounds when he died, aged fifty-one. The letters were from back to front, the first ones from the end of his stay then moving to the beginning. Near the end I found a letter from my great grandfather, Charlie's older brother, John M. Wing, which happens to be my name and my father's name. This letter, written in 1911, showed not embarrassment, but a dispute between brothers. A disowning. Something, perhaps, a tragic legend with an incorrect date might successfully hide for almost a century. While writing the poems in the last section, I was involved in some brotherly disputes of my own, so poems about that made their way in.

II

In each section of this book of poems, the reader will find, a version, a shading, an idea of the truth. My idea, in most cases. I learned writing comedy that the truth is rarely funny. The lie, the what-should-have-might-have-could-have-I-wish-had happened – that's what's funny. The CD, recorded in Winnipeg for Valentine's Day, 1999, is another example of that. So we have something based on a true story, inspired by imagined events, taken from the accounts of people who weren't there, the names changed to protect the lawyers.

Hegel wrote: *"It is therefore a misapprehension about reason when reflection is excluded from the true instead of being regarded as a positive moment of the absolute. It is reflection which makes the true a result, while also sublimating this opposition to its becoming, which is also quite simple and therefore not different from the form of the true which manifests itself in the guise of something simple. Rather, it is precisely this return into simplicity."*

Or, to put it another way: None of this is probably true.

JOHN WING JR.
29 NOVEMBER 2001
COZUMEL, MEXICO

...SINCERELY, FOR MY OWN PART, DO I WISH TO FIND AND KNOW THE TRUTH; BUT IF THIS BE TRUTH, WELL MAY SHE GUARD HERSELF WITH MYSTERIES AND COVER HERSELF WITH A VEIL. IF THIS BE TRUTH, MAN OR WOMAN WHO BEHOLDS HER CAN BUT CURSE THE DAY HE OR SHE WAS BORN.

CHARLOTTE BRONTE

ALL THE TRUTH IN THE WORLD ADDS UP TO ONE BIG LIE.

BOB DYLAN

ANOTHER NATURE

A POEM SHOULD BE EQUAL TO : NOT TRUE.
ARCHIBALD MACLEISH

RISEN

Bring back the dead comedians
from their unsmiling.
Train the harsh light upon them.
Judge them by the laughter
or the silence.

Bring back the dead comedians
from their long sleep-in.
Book them well in advance
for a proper fee, air and room.
Request the old routines, knowing
there's nothing new in the afterlife.

Bring back the dead comedians
from paradise, a thick-toweled hotel;
or hell, a nowhere Monday night
bar gig following the stripper.
Train the harsh light upon them
until they are warm.

27-28 JANUARY, 2001
LOS ANGELES - SAN JUAN

I WILL

I will whiten my teeth
for television, sleep with
a custom made mold in my mouth;
bite rubbery all night,
and awaken to the exquisite pleasure
of tearing it out.

I will smile at hosts
who hold up my unread book
and ask their lovely,
gossamer questions.

I will daub makeup
on my skin flaws, lament
each lost step or new sag
that pushes me out of the realm
of the young

I will feel the rush
of crowd-sound, time anticipation,
gulp the laugh-waves,
suck the marrow
out of what passes
for love.

✸ John Wing Jr.

FEBRUARY, 2001
VANCOUVER

FIRST KNOCK

I write this for tall, blond Joe
and his doorframe shoulders.
He could hit the ball a mile,
and score from anywhere.

And he loved a girl I also loved.
Married her, and I never saw them again.
We were all leaving town back then.

Joe and his shoulders and the girl I loved
went to Europe. My strange dreams
and I headed west to L.A.
And, suddenly, Joe died. I heard today.

Same age as I. Too young.
His children wonderingly sad. His wife
cut open for all to see.

His easy smile, wide as a freeway.
His large heart not as large
as once thought,
and now we know.

She's not coming back,
the girl I loved
who married tall, blond Joe,
who hit it far.
None of us are.

17 JULY, 2000
SAN JOSE - TUJUNGA, CA.

SECOND KNOCK

Two men, my age, husbands,
died suddenly last month.
Of course there were more
in the larger scheme,
but I knew these two.

One died in his sleep, healthy
until he closed his eyes.
The other, athletic, felt a strange
arm pain and just dropped dead.

Two. Gone.
These things always
seem to come
in threes.
Death's trinity.

The only problem is
I'm the only one who
knew both of them.

21 JULY. 2000.
TUJUNGA. CA.

BIRTHDAY POEM

Wishing this night might last –
or seem to last – longer.
So by morning this milestone
will be forgotten.

Wishing to live in a Toronto basement
writing poems, or even the novel
people laughingly assume is in me.

Wishing for a girl/woman
who moans at such proper times,
and makes me feel more the man/
boy.

Wishing my daughters weren't
growing up and away.

Wishing my wife were proud of me.

Wishing for a cigarette.

Wishing that sobriety wasn't
so damn *utter,* so perfectly
complete.

Wishing I didn't know
all I know
about me.

23 AUGUST. 1999
TORONTO - LOS ANGELES

CHOICES

Pool deck, one p.m.:
fat women in bikinis
waddle by. I should talk
I suppose. Fat men, tattooed
like whorehouse wallpaper,
not the slightest bit self conscious.
I suspect a tale
accompanies each one.
Either that, or prison.

Every now and then,
a woman for whom
the bikini was imagined
slides by. A jewel in her navel,
barbed wire surrounding one ankle.
My brisk imagination takes over.
I will write a poem about her.
Either that, or prison.

✶ John Wing Jr.

25 MAY. 2001
CARIBBEAN SEA.

TALK SHOW

I

She came to my dressing room
to say hello, mentioning she loved
the book, asking after certain ideas,
poems. She had read it more than once.

She was better looking in person,
(could she sense what I harboured?)
all soft curve and dark chocolate stare.
Her voice a warm wet cloth on my face.

And by now I was frightened
of being with her in all those living rooms
in such patent want. The camera may not
love me, but it knows me.

So I came out all excited, used
what was obvious. Screamed her name,
exhorting the audience to as well.
They all thought it was very funny.

Lucky to have humour there.
(She was flattered) Better
than moon-eyed rage or shame
to cloak such thudding.

II

He said, as warning,
The host has big tits.
Great, I said
No, he said, bigger than that.
Bigger than you can imagine.
I'm *serious.*

I tried imagining.

Are they real? I asked.
Yes, he replied. Real, huge, hard
to believe. *Do not* let the camera
catch you staring.

I promised.
Faithfully.

It was one of my best interviews.
I concentrated so hard on her eyes
I forgot what colour they were.

The camera caught me
a couple of times,
wishing.

Good job, he said,
driving me back
to the privacy of the hotel.

17 AUGUST, 2001
ST. CROIX, U.S.V.I.

BOOK SIGNING

Late in the hour she walks in;
the first girl I ever kissed.
Her name flashes instantly.
She is surprised that I know it.

It probably wasn't her first kiss.

I don't recall meeting her,
or asking her out.
Just that we were there
in her house, alone.

She kissed me in a doorway.
Her mouth opened,
and I felt the heat of her tongue
forever.

I wanted to kiss her again
so desperately the next time,
she thought it was funny.

She buys a book
and I sign it.
She introduces me to her husband,
whom she met that same year.

I remember his name, too.

3 MAY, 2001
ST. THOMAS, U.S.V.I.

INTERMISSION

She walked straight to me.
Her legs visible first, on the steps
coming down, then her face,
and the thought that I should know
who she was, that once I had.
She walked straight to me.

Speckled grey hair, unfashionable
glasses, body razor-thin, perfectly
pressed, and my uncertainty grew
until she was close enough to see
her eyes. And there it was: Face,
name, time, place, skin, smell
hair, youth, danger, *danger*, first.

She was everything
I didn't know, every wish
I still harbour of childish,
childless moments.

In easy conversation
she told me of her burnout
and hospitalization, and I related
my wife and children tales.
She was still married to the man
who had slept upstairs, unaware,
that night. A leg injury
prevented him from negotiating
the steps to say hello.

She seemed glad, almost relieved
to see me alone. Or not.
Maybe I was imagining so hard
that it projected upon her face.
Maybe that's what it was.

6 - 7 SEPTEMBER, 2001
BERMUDA

✦ John Wing Jr.

HIGH FIDELTY

A woman
(to me a girl)
without love to grease her smile.

I tell her my tales,
the well practiced ones.
(I still know all the pauses)

I can recall
with some effort,
being as young as she.

Easily I can imagine
everything of hers,
from forehead down.

I ask the priest,
Will this end? Will extreme
faith drown desire?

Will I see thorn-crowns and not breasts
under blouses? He shakes his head.
No help as usual.

I do not wish to be a sexual
sixteen anymore. Can my blood
be collared, the veins thinned?

I was sixteen when this woman
without love to grease her smile
was born. Without style or charm.

Anxious as a small fish.
She, an infant then,
would have hated me.

NOVEMBER. 1998 - JUNE. 1999
CARIBBEAN - CALIFORNIA

None of this is probably true

THE JOHN

Sometimes he asks them to call him names.

Stretched rack-taut on some phantasmic sensation,
he lifts his ostrich head and begs
for her verbal catlash.

Some instantly understand,
stage whispering the sweet
humiliation he so craves.

His mouth opens wide in scream-silence,
puckered breath escapes through unfilled apertures,
words prick his ears.

Some just don't get it.
He has to demonstrate.
Do an imitation of her doing it.
He hates that.

And sometimes, not often,
one gets it just perfect.
The rhythm of phrasethrust
thrustphrase.

And the voice becomes deeper
in his imagination, his excitement.
Unmistakable in his memory,
and he bursts forth,
pure, elemental,
accused.

19 - 30 JANUARY. 2000
TUJUNGA. CA.

OLD HABITS

It takes time,
but eventually
you find yourself
desperate for faces,
vowel sounds.
Yet uneasy
around them,
hyper-aware.

Movements that are real
and have never existed in your head
make you uncomfortable.

In the nocturnal hotel,
you remember a time
when you loved fantasies,
because they never woke you up
or threatened to expose you,
or wouldn't leave.

Now you'll sleep
with anyone
who'll hang around
after and talk,
chase the night
away with words

29 SEPTEMBER, 2000
WINNIPEG, MB.

WHAT I TELL YOU THREE TIMES IS TRUE

> Hell is truth seen too late.
> John Locke

THEN EVEN NOW

This unsloped land
of youth in its dark green glory
reminds me that I had no wish
to wander; no secret heartplace
full of punched tickets.
This was home.

Above the trees
in full summer dress is only sky
and unmilled windpaths,
like the quick air of nights
along the unstormed shore,
toes drowning in cool sand.

Just beginning
to understand that each mile
is a different world, despite
changes in storefront
and streetlamp, this flat
lakeside will always be mine.

The colours take
the seasoned place now. Barn-red
and field-yellow between tree-green,
with sky-blue and moon-white.
And they zoom by, springing
leaks in the imagination.

But I did leave
the long grass, though the maples
and walnuts dropped leaves
to lead me back, sun and moon
waving as they passed,
I forgot how slowly night falls.

None of this is probably true

And return now
only to mourn the blurred faces.
This mountainless land could be called
then, even now. Not for what is lost
but what is past. Names calling out
from stones. The sound of water.

26 - 30 JUNE, 1999
DETROIT - PORT HURON - PHOENIX

ELBOW-ROTIC

Perfection only comes in elbows.

Bones squared and pointed, jaw-
breaking power, weaponry, reminders,
and the most peculiar body zap
if you strike them in the wrong
(right) place.

Good for a thousand household uses.

Adjustable for embracing, arm-
wrestling, reach point crook thrust
parry swing salute.

Without the elbow we wouldn't have words

like *headlock*, or *chokehold*.

And it will bend as often as you can blink,
and never lose its spring.

Without elbows, poets
would have to write with their mouths.

None of this is probably true ✣

22 JULY. 2000
TUJUNGA. CA.

LICENSE RENEWAL

Reading poetry in the day-long line
at the DMV. Occasionally looking up
at the sound of bells or whistles,
the great sigh-movement of the line.

We stare at the employees,
never our fellow linemates.
Eyes flit about them, never resting,
like hummingbirds.

The body heat, the studied patience;
we are like refugees, showing no anxiety
or desperation. Then the bell that is ours
rings, and we disappear to other lines.

When done, our refugee-photo
taken, we depart the large, inhabited room
for the much smaller one
that is empty until we fill it.

All men are islands,
entire of their cars.

21 - 22 JULY, 2000
TUJUNGA, CA.

HOLLYWOOD

Underlying ecstasies abound
here.

The tall green buildings are mistaken
for rock outcroppings.

The grass is yellow from disuse.

Everyone is wearing glasses,
staring straight ahead.

No one speaks.

Each leaving
is an old beginning.

Each loss steeped in false hope.

The elbow up under the ribs
suggests swift movement before

rage.

24 MARCH. 2000
WINNIPEG. MB.

THE CHEETAH

Sometimes I think you told me everything
when I wasn't listening.

Why is everyone so fat?

Short snakes wriggle from offices
into saloons at the end of days.

Wet gunpowder drips from the ceiling.

Sometimes I think
I've been asleep for centuries.

The government is worried
about how fat everyone is,
and has promised to do nothing.

Marriage is at last protected.
Disease is immoral.

And here I am. Sitting.
Watching.

The cheetah will be extinct before
another sentence is composed,

and will return as a fast car
that trips and strangles other cars.

✸ John Wing Jr.

19 FEBRUARY, 2000
MIAMI - LOS ANGELES

IMMORTALITY ON THE ROAD TO EDMONTON

A row of baby
scotch pines
line the highway.

A For Sale sign
at the end
of this futured
fence.

Trees are the hope,
like the children
we pray will grow tall,
but never leave.

None of this is probably true ❋

10 AUGUST. 2000
ALBERTA

LETTER TO THE CHILDREN FROM THE ROAD

There were very important weeks,
singular days, soft perfect moments
I wasn't there.

I often told you to look for me
inside the longhouse
of your remembering,
and I would appear.

But did I?

Or was it just the appointed hours;
the symbolic Sunday or Monday
when cars and buses and planes
delivered me, bone-tired and bleary,
from that far away?

Long after you needed.

After the story had passed
from green to grey,
and new ideas had sprung
without me.

John Wing Jr.

13 DECEMBER, 2000
WINNIPEG, MB.

RACHEL, AGED EIGHT

Through the classroom window
she appears so assured, adult.
Childhood is falling
from her face.
The hesitation is gone.
Innocence lingers,
but soon enough,
crimes will sharpen her.

FULMINATE

My daughter is about to explode,
The world is target-rich
and she is fully armed.
fire and percussion   mortar
grenade

She will be beautiful;
will become breath,
the destroyer.
incendiary   defoliant
Bouncing Betty

Her brain will begin
to grasp concepts
and strangle them.
fragmentation   scattershot
delayed action

Her liquid nitrogen eyes
will match the body to come.
Heads will turn just before blindness.
shape charge   penetration
fire in the hole

Some she'll bring home,
eager in their pre-injury daze.
Unbandaged, nicknamed.
 wadcutter   hollow point
 dum dum

Take careful steps, those
who would attempt to defuse
her. She is ticking.
nitro   napalm
anti-personnel

My daughter is about to explode.
I will turn my head and welcome
blindness at her flashpoint.
*vapourized   radiated
ground zero*

5 AUGUST, 2000
TUJUNGA, CA.

None of this is probably true ✤

NUMEROLOGY

She still wells up at burnt waffles,
pumps tears at injustice, but writes
poems, too. And jokes. Reads
Harry Potter in hard covers, asks me
what arithomancy means.

The weeks I'm home, she sneaks
from bed late to sit with me,
or asks for fresh water, twinkling
when I suggest ulterior motives.

She won't cut her hair, cries
in great pain when it's brushed,
dresses in her nouveau-ridiculous
way, about which I attempt to say
nothing. Thanks me for her own
room, a foolish almost forgotten promise
I managed to keep. And I wonder
what the numbers will tell.

At nine, she has a larger world
than I will ever know. Walking her
to the school gate, standing at the fence
like a convict, watching her go.
With each step she is farther away.

✦ John Wing Jr.

19 - 20 NOVEMBER, 2001
SUNLAND, CA.

MOTHER AT THE AIR CANADA CENTER

She smiles and takes it all in
at a glance, even though
it's been over thirty years since
a Bobby Hull slapshot sailed
over net and glass at Olympia
and smashed her shoulder.

I suppose attending hockey games
took a back seat after that. After
she knew *exactly* how goalies felt
when the stick rose for that splitsecond
above shoulder. She didn't need
to go anymore. Like World War II,
Europe, marriage, five children, the death
of her parents, a car accident, and angioplasty;
been there. Done that.

Even the fact that I asked Dad first,
knowing he'd say no thanks,
didn't bother her. No sir.
Riding the King streetcar down
to the new rink, her granddaughter
bouncing with excitement, she must
have recalled her own father, snap-
brim fedora just so, taking her
to the Forum to see the Rocket play.
Wild-eyed Maurice barreling down
the wing as the crowd surged and shook
with glee when he put it in.

Even now, watching TV hockey,
she sometimes lets go that tiny *shriek*
that sheds her years and puts her back
in fabled, mid-century Montreal
where she saw Jackie Robinson play
for the Royals, and the unmasked
Jacques Plante sliding across to make
the big save.

None of this is probably true

Mothers were strong when I was young.
Childbirth was another day at the office.
120 mile-an-hour slapshots to the collarbone
were taken without complaint; the bragging-rights
bruise shown endlessly to all the neighbourhood
boys we brought home. I wonder if we ever
thanked her for the status such things bestow.

Snug in her seat, she leans down
to her American born grandchild
attending her very first game, and anxious
to tell her Nonni all about hockey. She listens
carefully to the little girl, smiling. No one is
as beautiful as my mother at the Air Canada Center.
Everything she has ever known
travels with her.

9 OCTOBER, 2001
OFF HISPIANOLA, CARIBBEAN SEA

TWO IS NONE

THESE SEEM THE FACTS.
ALISTAIR MACLEOD

BLUES FROM A SMALL ROOM

I am standing naked
in this room,
and you
can't hear me.

I am sliced
in a hundred places,
and my blood
runs silently.

These are the lies
dressed as love songs.

This is the sound
of your stare.

None of this is probably true ✤

10 DECEMBER. 2000
WINNIPEG. MB.

NEW PAJAMAS

The new pajamas aren't right.
She cries tears. The sleeves
are too tight at the wrist.

They'll stretch, I say,
ridiculously, unaware
that it's over already.
The too-strangling-tight
tear-inducing pajamas
are finished, never
to be worn again.

Later, when she safely
sleeps in old, loose-wristed
pajamas, you and I sit
across from each other.

You cry tears, recalling
something I said yesterday.
I am all ignorant innocence,
but it would be more
than foolish to disbelieve you.

Only anger seems to quicken
the blood now. Suspicion,
resentment, these are our bullets.

You cry again.
I want to say,
We'll stretch,
because it occurs to me.

♣ John Wing Jr.

TAKEN DOWN AND USED IN EVIDENCE

When she says
"I don't feel lust for you anymore,"
as though it is as natural
as grey hair or ingrown nails;
as though we are old
the way our parents always seemed to be...

And you stop
eating snacks, quit
smoking, start
running to nowhere
40 minutes a day on a treadmill,
splaying yourself over
modern torture racks to achieve
visible bulge, to become
hard against her lustlessness.

And find, toned and sculpted,
that it isn't you she doesn't feel
lust for. It is lust she does not feel.
"Maybe when I'm fifty," she says.
(eight years)

You wonder if something
you could say would hurt
as much as this hurts.
But such cruelty would be deliberate,
and hers is not.
She is merely stating a fact.
Something has left her,
and you can't bring it back
or even take it personally.

Later, she notices
your sudden depression,
and suggests you return
to therapy.

MAY/JUNE, 1999

NEW SKINS

That we have separated
from one to distant ones
is true. Although we share
it alone, as a secret giggled
into simpler sleep.

That my organs are on display
is no longer fascinating.

That her reluctance to exhume
old pain is her own business.

That more is not said now.
Love has become
like the gardening,
the sweeping,
the making of beds,
a service.

Something to be put away
in its proper place
when guests come.

Smiles are worn like evening clothes

That it is not an ending
or a breaking of us
is also true. A moving
of minds to new perches
undesired by both.
A change.
A recognition.

25 JUNE. 2000
TUJUNGA. CA.

TIMEBENDS

Sometimes love cannot be found
in anger's well. Scattered among
the insult shards, the wounds
old and fresh.

Sometimes love is as simple
as feeling your eyes upon me.
Seeing me again.

Sometimes wishes become
great surf-polished stones
that weigh us down with...
*I wish he didn't...I wish
it wasn't so...I wish it was
more,* or *less,* but
not *this.*

Sometimes there is nothing
as perfect as you reading
in your painted garden, even
though knowing I am watching
would spoil the sound.

Sometimes I want to discover
you without expectations, with
only possibilities. Sometimes
I want to hide the fear and travel
back to your unknown.

Sometimes I want to present
myself to you, unscarred,
unthinking, all senses
hungry.

Sometimes a bone must be broken
before light can pass through it.

21 AUGUST. 2000
CALGARY. AB.

None of this is probably true

FANTASIES

She says little,
almost nothing.
A rare phrase is
forced in laughter.

She is body.
Silent pleasure.
Nothing during,
nothing after.

No suggestions
mar this dancing.
One's too fast,
and one's too slow.

Eyes shut, each one
lost in wishes.
His: just *tell me.*
Hers: just *know.*

19 AUGUST. 2001
SAN JUAN - FT. LAUDERDALE - LOS ANGELES

INVINCIBLE

Often I have wished to find imperfection in you.
Some chink, some secret want, betrayal
of words, ridiculous kindness in the true
sense. A romantic notion perhaps, frail
and naked as a child by a toy display.

I have known hiders, little-box people, but they
were easy as diaries with small
locks that a strong breath would open. Just to say
the theory unsnapped them, exposed all
their weak treasures. No such bullet makes you blink.

Have known hell in your silence, heaven in your wink.
Fired love from a cannon, watched it miss
the mark and land unexploded. Still, I think
beneath your armour-plate lies a forced kiss,
somewhere. When I hear you laugh I envy the joke.

None of this is probably true ✣

5 - 20 NOVEMBER. 2001
SUNLAND. CA.

HALF THE KNOWN WORLD

There is no interim, no space
between what we know and believe
and what mystifies, shocks, turns heads,
changes everything. Instead
there is a country, ten countries,
an empire. The Mongol Empire – 13th
century – stretching from the Bering
to the Mediterranean. Half the known world.
But what did they really know?

Across the trackless Gobi
I came to your gates. You refused
me entry, fought savagely and still do,
knowing now if you capitulate, I'll
have to kill everyone, as an example.
It has become a test of strength, of will.
I come, but you can feel me tiring, more
unsure. You ask for nothing again and again.
I ride from one end of you to the other.

I tell you I have sent for reinforcements
and you smile. We are the only ones left,
you say, calling my bluff. I don't want
to believe you anymore. You hold
the last thing I am sure of in your hand,
rolling it slowly between your fingers.
Everything I don't know surrounds us.
Horses' hooves can be heard far off,
tattooing the night. *Hurry.* Convince me.

✦ John Wing Jr.

12 SEPTEMBER, 2001
BERMUDA

EVEREST

Your ankle is just a beginning,
a foothold. Slowly, conserving
oxygen, I traverse the perfect
pitch of your calf, landmarking
spots for a return. The corniched
side of your knee is formidable.
I opt for an inside passage
and, wind-sheltered, I nuzzle rest
in the ridge below your dauntingly
sheer thigh. The radio crackles
news. A storm building above.
I leave my extra canister and head
toward the fissure I still can see.
The light fades.
The wind comes in gasps.
I feel my way.

None of this is probably true ✤

6 - 8 SEPTEMBER. 2001
BERMUDA - NY

UNTIL THEN

Sometimes I wonder what happens
to all the little poems I've written
for your birthdays and our anniversaries.

I wonder where you've cached them.
Under a suitable cairn of clothing,
in a small drawer with other longhand mementoes.

Are they ever reread? Do you even
like poetry? Perhaps you think I dash
these off in lieu of a real gift.

You might scoff, or chill your gaze at this,
but how could you understand? You have never
glimpsed yourself in the mirror of my eyes,

or felt the great pang of unworthiness;
the knowledge that I will not unlock you,
open your little drawers, make you safe and soft.

Secrets are not unspoken, they are
habit-hidden, kept *under* or *behind* and almost
forgotten. I am here never to tell you what I know.

Standing in the doorway tonight,
watching you undress,
I will think only of this.

✦ John Wing Jr.

30 MAY - 1 JUNE, 2001
MIAMI - COZUMEL

DESCRIBING HER IN TERMS OF SEA LIFE

Mythic as the white whale.
Often harpooned, never taken.

Shark-sleek, she can go
only forward, nonstop to the next
the next the next thing

Swordfish-stubborn, she takes
all your line and leaves.

Pure yellowfin, she hangs back.
her guard up as she sleeps.

Salmon-bright, she waits
for the brown bear to leave.
Life is upstream.

Oyster-perfect. Long ago
someone pried her open
and left a note in place of the pearl.

None of this is probably true ❖

8 - 16 SEPTEMBER. 2001
BERMUDA - NY - LOS ANGELES

HOMECOMING

There is still time, he thinks,
to make her love me. To show
why such love is deserved.

I'll be home Friday, he writes,
and she counts the days.
Two good ones left.

Before falling asleep, she decides,
his first night home, I will make
love to him.

I'll even fake orgasm, she thinks.
A big loud one. So he'll know.
So he won't have to ask.

Instead they have their version
of a fight; where they sit in silent
fear of what could be said.

Give it time, she thinks.

He writes *fuck you*
in her journal.

✦ John Wing Jr.

28 - 30 NOVEMBER, 2001
CARIBBEAN - MEXICO - LOS ANGELES

NONE OF THIS IS PROBABLY TRUE

ALL OF THIS IS MADNESS. BUT IT IS TRUE.
LEO TOLSTOY

INTERVIEW

...ACQUIRED MADNESS OF A TYPE KNOWN ONLY TO INTIMATE MEMBERS OF LONG DEAD SOCIETIES...

Not the question — *not* the question
not the answer
the time the place   or
the thing is
this is
this is what happened
what happened was
I'm not here
you didn't see me
you didn't find me
or hear of me being
you didn't love me like
I needed nobody
fucking *nobody* did
underscore that for emphasis you —
you me

Who was I when I was?
Yes and did you see me
where was I
acting the loud brash boy
of the party
voicestoned
fleshdrunk
did you think you knew me?

Were you there when I crucified myself
the fourteenth time?
Were you ever under
the illusion that I could be
saved repaired bandaged juryrigged
into husbandry and fathershould
so I might repent repeat
the incorrects and force others into ritual
liver damage?

None of this is probably true

This is not the way
the truth and the slight
the carapace the solving
of nothing no mystery
here this is showbiz
and it must go on
true love never dies
until something better comes
along in your face you know
the glass tells you true self-
loathing is what never dies
until sleep or will death even
dent this?

Not the question – *not*
the question black pit boy
notebookish man of letters
and telling blinks fuck
you me you too

. . .PERHAPS HEREDITARY PARANOIA FROM MATER-
NAL SIDE. FATHER'S FAMILY ALL DEAD AND NO
ASYLUM...

PREFACE

None of this is probably true.

True things come as infants.
Slow and painful, down
a narrow canal.

And you are just beginning
to realize the dark emerging
circle is a head
when the shoulder slips through.

And, like a cannonball,
truth is born, dizzying
in its speed.

20 MARCH, 2001
VANCOUVER - SASKATOON

TWO HISTORIES

I

Legend has it

History is legend
printed on good paper.

Conquerors couldn't write.
They hired ghosts
to fancy-up their tell-tales.

Truth is

History is a bully.
Pushes its way into books.
Elbows out facts. Makes
hearsay a virtue.

It's been said

Flattens truth
the way ranchers
clear forests into fields.

And the real become homeless,
undispersed, and die out.

Soon everyone
believes the fields
were always there.

II

I've heard tell

Family legend
is after-dinner history.
Pleasing tales to amuse new lovers,

or frighten old ones.

A way of being special,
or just more than piss-poor
pig-ignorant farmers
one or two generations back.

No.
They were artists, life-peers,
even a whiff of royalty somewhere.

They say

And it was not insanity,
he was eccentric.
And if anyone ever deserved
to get shot, she did.

So I've been told

Someone will always live
to embellish the tale.

Word is

So be careful.
Investigate at your peril

None of this is probably true ♣

the census records
and the names
of the landed gentry.

Remember the flat truth
is all that awaits you.

or so the story goes.

27 NOVEMBER, 1999
MIAMI - LOS ANGELES.

SECRETS

My grandfather hated a few things.
His given name, emotional display,
laziness, black people,
and what I did for a living.

Searching out family resting places,
I once asked him about his Uncle Charlie.
Subject of much rumour.

But Grandpa wouldn't speak of it.
Stone refused. *"We don't talk about Charlie,"*
was all he would say.

I showed him the photograph
of the five Wing brothers, circa 1900,
his own father dead center in pince-nez
and the haughty mustache of the day.
"Charlie's the bearded one, right?"

He turned away, as though
it was somehow classified.
As though 70 years before I asked
he had signed a pledge of secrecy.

"I only want to know where he's buried," I said.

He lit a shaking cigarette.
Looked right at me.

"Have you thought about going back to school?" he asked.

WINTER 2000 - AUTUMN 2001
LOS ANGELES

DWELLINGS

I don't live in California.

I live in Sarnia, crammed
with 19 years of knowledge
that never grows or dies.

I live in Woodstock, near
the old folks home Grampa
kept escaping from.

I live in Windsor, where
everyone who knew my Dad had me over,
and virginal girls taught me
all the don'ts.

I live through Toronto, in
one-rooms just off downtown.
Rich in my understanding of avenues,
and never old, even in despair.

I live in the London Asylum
at the beginning of the century, watching
my great-great uncle Charlie
die of tuberculosis.

I tell him I'm only dreaming.
But he doesn't believe me.

14 MAY, 2001
TUJUNGA, CA.

CLUES

This is all there is
left of a man

A seven year medical file

I look through it again
without understanding
what everyone didn't want to know.

From an era
in which no one talked
about such things.

There were only the farms,
the crops, the seasons,
the weather.

Hard to believe
there was even language then.
The unspoken was all
the rage.

MARCH. 2001

INNOVATOR

The doctor, a Whitman-ite
has *Leaves of Grass* placed
in every room.

Some copies survive yet
in collections. A recent auction
advertised one as 'never
having been opened'.

One would almost be afraid.
The years of keening
absorbed into the pages.
The osmotic paranoia
that is now *Song Of Myself.*
Crossing Brooklyn Ferry infused
with the screams of the drowning.

Legend has it
one ate his copy
cover to cover,
and shit perfect poetry
for a month.

UNCLE CHARLIE'S BLUES

No, I'm not happy here.
Of course I am.
You don't know.

I never meant to hurt her,
did I? It was my brothers,
and the lightning, don't forget
that, the flashes.

You say.
You say she's dead.
But she came by. She did.
I *spoke* with her. Last night
You don't know.
In my room. She told me
I was fine. Just fine. And
I was happy here. She
wouldn't lie. She wouldn't.
Why would she?

I don't want to go outside.
No. I don't want to work
on the grounds. No.
I don't *want* to be trusted.

Well, I hate the tree
outside my room. The elm, yes.
I wish it would die.
It shakes and rattles, and the branches
sneak through the window at night
and try to poke out my eyes.
Both of them.

None of this is probably true ✤

7 - 9 SEPTEMBER, 2001
BERMUDA - NY

You've *never* been electrocuted.
I have. I *have*. You don't know.
What? What?
I can hear what you say
to yourself, you know.
I can.

1305

Rodney Aug 28/11

Dr Robertson

Dear Sir

I received a letter on the 7th inst requesting clothing for Chas. Wing. I am not responsible for his clothing so I think there must be some mistake. He has been given articles of clothing at Christmas but I did not expect to cloth him. Hoping this will be satisfactory

Yours
John Wing

None of this is probably true

JUXTAPOSITION

On those days
when secrets emerge
from long hiding,
like weather patterns
meeting to form great storms,
everything must be aligned just so.

It could be the hundredth time
that story your father told you about his crucible
goes through your head,
or even the ten thousandth time,
but consummation comes,
and the tiny, perfect lie pops out,
the Johnstown flood behind it.

It could be
at the one room college apartment
of a girl, talking about
a mutual friend you never see anymore.
She makes tea in the alcove kitchen
as you glance around the room, your eyes
stopping momentarily on the unmade,
girl-laced bed. She asks how you take your tea.

You look at the bed again
and know everything.

20 MARCH. 2001
VANCOUVER - SASKATOON

ORPHANS

Certain things have come to light,
such as my brother's imagined stand
against his own addiction.

After not using for some months
and drinking like a fish, he declared,

"I miss heroin *profoundly.*"

"But I'm *not* an addict."

My father, in his sixties
when his father died at age 92,
calling me and saying,

"I'm an orphan."

"And you are not to come to the funeral."
"It's too far and you can't afford it."

The last order I would foolishly obey.
In my thirties, on the brink
of fatherhood myself.

But I'll come to my brother's service.
When not being addicted finally
stops his blue veins.

I'll be an orphan myself by then.

Missing everyone profoundly.

21 APRIL. 1999
TUJUNGA. CA.

PREDICTION

I predict that nuance
will eventually disappear.

We will not speak again
without underthought, hear
without ticking the crime-list.

There is too much water.

Love is an empty wallet
full of litanies.

In the word-crossfire,
nobody wants to be seen ducking.

There is too much.

There is

too.

24 MARCH, 2001
WINNIPEG - VANCOUVER

REAL REASONS

This room is so small.

I don't phone.
And each time he does,
once a year or so now,
he subtly reproaches me
for my forgetfulness.

But, of course,
my ignoring of his life
is deliberate.

Once I was interested
in making him see my view
of his choices, to the point
where I said something
he will never forget.

It comes up,
once a year or so now.
He tells me again
how he never thinks of it
and holds no grudges.

He knows it's not forgetfulness.
He thinks I don't like him,
which is actually easier.

Real reasons are for people
with less to lose.

This room is so small.
It could never contain my ego.

26 - 28 FEBRUARY. 2001
CARIBBEAN SEA

None of this is probably true

THE LOVER'S SONG

Nights alone in small and smaller rooms.
I have a cathode's entertainment, some idea
of life performed on grander scales, pages filled
with words, mine to decrypt, with evil thoughts
as though I were invisible, memories I have slanted
into lies, and my old friend, diseased but grinning
widely, assuring me of her constant love.

Because of her, I have known certain streets
too well. The blistered concrete, stubborn weeds
that burst through cracks. The crumbled brick
facades and greywood porches I have seen
in my disheveled wanderings. There I'll find her
and we'll return to small and smaller rooms.
She'll stab me bloody as I bathe.

We will float along the papered corridors;
amnesiacs to simple pain and giant hatred,
secure in our special, secret knowledge. I will deny
of course, ever meeting her, swear to no
apostled partnership, curse her as she turns
me into rock and builds her church upon me,
veined with gold.

And if they ever find me, sofa-stiff in my peeling
room, tube-lit in comic white, will they know
that I left *her*? Fearing the perfect dreams
she gave me, drowning in the bath she drew, holding
my own head under until she cried. Not worthy,
I watched her slip away toward the naked bulb.
Small and smaller.

5 - 6 JUNE, 2001
HAITI - JAMAICA

RIVALS

Someone will make a pretty story
out of our foolishness, our brotherly
hatred. My daughters, perhaps,
or their sons, if it matters,
will clean the tale.

They will say it was over a woman.

The heavy-breasted girl of yours
I bedded after you left, or she left,
or during. Or the one you nailed
who wrote a letter to your girlfriend,
ending both.

I wrote the letter, they will say.

Or the father we disagreed upon,
the love I made sure you never got,
the jealousy of achievement,
the unforgiven talents, the empty boxes
we tossed to each other as gifts.

I'd had enough of brothers when you arrived,
they will say.

I failed to awaken you and you missed
the train to college. I ratted you out
when you stole that bicycle. I never told
anyone how great you were. I sided with others.
You never forgave me for not forgiving you.
I took your colouring book.

Surely my literary-minded daughters
will concoct a scenario
even a biographer could believe.

None of this is probably true

Your biographer.
No, mine.

I found your girlfriend an abortionist,
accompanied her, paid the bill,
and murdered your child. I wanted
to be the first father, fearing you would
knock up some slutty conquest and outstrip me.
Your careless potency was legend. So
I intervened, convinced her
to kill it.

They might say that, you know.

"Synthesize it into your poetry,"
You said. A classy *fuck you* just
before announcing you would never
speak to me again again. Our feud
approached thirty years now,
and like bones in a closet, the origins
are difficult to recognize. Someone
will explain it someday, after we're dead.

Or maybe I'll outlive you,
you little prick.

RECIPE

Revenge is a dish
best eaten cold. Freeze it,
thaw it, slice thinly,
serve with cabbage, or crow.

Some prefer their vengeance
warm, with lightly browned
shallots and fresh grated parmesan.

Sauteed justice is simple; heat
up the olive oil, then throw in
your green feelings, for two
minutes only!

Then revenge is sweet
and crisp as perfect
asparagus spears.

Bake resentment slowly
at 400 degrees, on half hour
for each year harboured,
so it remains tender.

Deep fry anger until crunchy.
Stew in own juices.
Season to taste.

None of this is probably true ✽

ROOTS OF INSOMNIA

I remember everything but dreams.
Can follow anything except directions.
Late at night I prowl. Stand at the window
watching the grey street for coyotes,
trotting up the hill.
Making the dogs bark.

I have stolen pianos
and sold them for rent and booze.
I have stood in a long addict-line
until my feet hurt from needles.
I have brooded over insults
until they became bullets.

The night deepens. I have checked
sleeping children and set the motion lights.
I remember everything but dreams.
Always get lost in the shortcuts.
I stalk inspiration, while beside me
a tall glass fills with darkness.

♣ John Wing Jr.

13 MAY. 2001
TUJUNGA. CA.

We should not take offence when people hide the truth from us, since so often we hide it from ourselves.

La Rochefoucauld

ACKNOWLEDGEMENTS

Some of these poems appeared in *Generation 2000*, and *The University Of Windsor Review*.

Michael Power provided the research on the London Asylum, which inspired me at the outset. He and his wife, Kathleen are both excellent readers who have given unselfishly of their time. Marty Gervais, Phil Hall, and John Ditsky are also invaluable readers and friends. The University of Windsor honoured me with a writer-in-residence week, which was one of the great weeks of my life, and I am indebted to Katherine Quinsey and everyone at the English department, especially Tom Dilworth, Dale Jacobs, Heidi Jacobs, Susan Holbrook, and Natalia Khomenko. John B. Lee, Roger Bell, and Don Coles provided me with hospitality and excellent advice.

Thanks to Howard Aster, renaissance man, and everyone at Mosaic Press.

The women who make my life what it is are Dawn, Rachel, Isabel, Angela, Paula, & Alexa.

MEMBER OF SCABRINI MEDIA

Quebec, Canada
2002